Scenes and Speculations

poems by

T.P. Bird

Finishing Line Press
Georgetown, Kentucky

Scenes and Speculations

Copyright © 2021 by T.P. Bird
ISBN 978-1-64662-437-9 First Edition
All rights reserved under International and Pan-American Copyright Conventions. No part of this book may be reproduced in any manner whatsoever without written permission from the publisher, except in the case of brief quotations embodied in critical articles and reviews.

ACKNOWLEDGMENTS

Poems published in *Relief Quarterly, Penwood Review, Poetry quarterly, BoomerLit, Common Ground Review, Miller's Pond,* and *Tiny Seed.*

Publisher: Leah Huete de Maines
Editor: Christen Kincaid
Cover Art: Photo by Konstantine Trundayev on Unsplash
Author Photo: Sarah Bird
Cover Design: Elizabeth Maines McCleavy

Printed in the USA on acid-free paper.
Order online: www.finishinglinepress.com
also available on amazon.com

Author inquiries and mail orders:
Finishing Line Press
P. O. Box 1626
Georgetown, Kentucky 40324
U. S. A.

Table of Contents

Scenes

Notes from a Summer Park 1

Home in Summer 3

Lines for an Outhouse Whose Name Was Blue 5

A Small Elegy for My Mother 6

The Marvelous Wedge and the Transit Hero 7

Visit to My Father's Hometown 8

While Atop an Unnamed Arcadian Hill 9

While Sitting Atop a Catlin Hill Meadow in Early Autumn 11

Sugar Hill Triptych 12

Washington Park 14

Cinnamon Lake Soundings 17

On the Trail to Dunning Pond 18

Field Notes While Walking Buck Hollow Road in Early June 19

Speculations

Four Speculations of a Contrary Nature 21

Do the Ghosts of Old Farmers Still Watch the Weather? 31

Out of Step 33

Orientation to Life among the Ruins 35

Scenes

NOTES FROM A SUMMER PARK

I've come to this small city park
to read and wait, perhaps to write
what a summer of sun, sights and

sounds has to offer a poet. Kids'
shouting from the public swimming
pool: ultraviolet rays and heat mix

with chlorine wetness to remind me
of summer days as a small boy,
plunging into the cool water of *my*

local pool with no muzzled sounds of
joy, nor hiding my glee, my pleasure,
as I shouted as loud as possible so

my voice would be heard among all
the shouts of all the summers to come
                beyond my own.

Sneakers, shorts, a stripped-off
t-shirt and a cap turned backwards
jump off a ten speed bike and race

to the net: a youth has come to the
local court; he arrives in the fore-
shadowing of an entire life to come.

Shooting baskets is a boy's practice
at putting things in their proper
place—later as a man appearing

successful and coming away with
acclaim. Yet, it's *this* moment that's
most important as a black kid in

Scenes

sweats, red kerchief over his head,
joins the shooter—merging into a
game of one-on-one. More youths

come to this training ground where
youths sharpen skills for a hero's
world. The vigor of youth flashes

across the court like lasers. Arms
and legs pump and drive toward
a glory only they can understand.

An aging man's legs are cramped
from sitting and watching under
the shade of a large maple tree.

His glory is sharing this summer
day in a small city park with other
                        human beings.

Scenes

HOME IN SUMMER

Curtains blow about in a light
breeze. The moving air picks up
their dusty scent—adding to its

already acquired fragrance.
Outside my window, voices rise
and fall like waves breaking in

on my inner conversation. Piano
music buoys from the other room—
a teen daughter is practicing for

a coming recital. Next door a pup
barks in crazy canine excitement;
its yap mixes with human babel

in a dissonant chorus, not at all
resonating with the piano's tones.
Sounds and smells have become a

kind of motion, like currents in a
river they mix with my thoughts.
Or, perhaps, they are like the tidal

sea where fishermen drop their
nets in the water. My faculties are
that net—catching what I need,

and what is not favored—pulling
into my little boat called life—
distractions as well as pleasures.

And so, to fully delight myself
in a time of inconsistency, I copy
in my notebook a special poem:

Home in Summer

"Home is fun in the summer,

Scenes

*because we go swimming or
wading or even reading. I
love reading, it is interesting
because you think it's real,
but it's just letters and words."*

—Sarah Jane Bird, (age nine)

Scenes

LINES FOR AN OUTHOUSE WHOSE NAME WAS BLUE

Where the Blue Room used to be
is a badly blurred photograph
of purple earth and static grass.
Never again will I hear the shuddering
thwack of its closing door, nor peer
out upon helplessly sunburned people,
trapped beneath the frosted pane,
where a horsefly made its home
among some very old paint chips.

One night some clowns chose
to undo Blue's classic lines,
and set Old Blue afire.

I'll never know the persons who
struck the match that made Blue
a sacrifice to their god of ignorance.
I guess they never realized
that Old Blue would have been
the perfect spot to get their heads
back in the right place.

Scenes

A SMALL ELEGY FOR MY MOTHER
—For Rita Saxe Bird (1917-1987)

She stayed apart her final days,
keeping to herself any dark
thoughts of dying and death.
Suffering was a conversation
never shared—despite its stark
loneliness and isolation. Instead,
she let her reticence descend
like a small blanket of grace over
the familiar space of shared lives.
And here it lay until . . .

at the end of this imposed exile:
A steely and defiant German-Irish
jaw slackened, awaiting death,
her usual tough voice of sufficiency
softened by words of gratitude,
tribute the only color in her face.

And finally: a husband, numb and
bowed at the foot of her hospital
bed, her grown son wading into
the fading presence of his mother's
retreating gaze.

Scenes

THE MARVELOUS WEDGE AND THE TRANSIT HERO

flying towards me like an arrow—
a marvelous wedge of Canada
geese, southbound in a bright,

clear October sky. On they come—
until, directly over my head, an
invisible hand pulls loose a hidden

string and many birds tumble out
of flying formation like potatoes
dropped from a gunny sack.

After a few commanding honks,
they obediently move back in
a revised wedge and soon their

flight path shifts directly south
and into the sun; the big birds,
disappear into the light.

—

At this convergence of bird and
man a strange notion occupies my
thoughts, a gentle hubris dilating

my ego. I imagine this marvelous
wedge chose me as a marker along
their way; my upturned, inquiring

face and acute eye alerting them
to a critical course adjustment.
What a marvel is this allocated

                life on earth.

Scenes

VISIT TO MY FATHER'S HOMETOWN

Driving the back roads and haunts
of his early years, my father and I
entered the town of his birth via

the 'back way'—the main road
before US 220 was built with steam
shovels and the force of mens' sweat.

We passed the house where his life-
long friend, George K., lived as a boy
in knee pants—an abandoned and

crumbling shell with faded yellow
paint and a sagging front porch—from
which his mother yelled at the three

brothers who always got her son into
childhood trouble. Though our windows
were open, we drove by too fast to hear

the ghostly echo of her angry words,
nor the brothers' crazy laughter as they
ran down the hilly road towards home.

Following the way, old houses appeared
where neighbors once lived with names
now mostly forgotten, occupied now by

strangers with different sets of memories.
My father recalled a gnarled old apple tree,
now fallen down behind a strong stone

wall that once fenced in grazing sheep;
no animal now stood in the tall grass of
the empty pasture. In his memory, those

apples were sweeter than Eden's own
fruit. Saint Basil's, where a young boy
rang the church bell three times a day,

Scenes

was a mandatory stop—almost sacred
to an old man's sentiment, the sting
of a nun's rap of knuckles still felt.

Standing on the cemetery hill behind
the church, his young self ran wild again
through the town like a passing storm.

Scenes

WHILE ATOP AN UNNAMED ARCADIAN HILL

Standing atop this treeless hill,
the early June sun clear and hot—
a breeze cools my skin against
the unaccustomed warmth after a
northern winter and a cool spring.

A tractor works hard somewhere
on a nearby, unseen knoll. It chugs
and snorts like a mechanical ox
against its yoke—its unsung driver
quite oblivious to my wanderings.

Yellow wild-flowers dot the ground
at my feet and well beyond the swell
of my breath. Tiny insects dive and
swirl around me—King Kong on the
'state' building of their pastoral city.

At a moderate distance and across
a small dale, an appealing tree line
runs atop a long ridge. From here
they spread a pencil width apart.
On either side, the rise is open turf.

A strange urge captivates me—
a longing to rest beneath the
shadowy coolness of those trees.
Perhaps, deep thoughts & sublime
verse await me there to discover.

Surely, the ridge's grass is greener,
a mind likely to be clearer, more
discerning. Oh, wanderlust ranging
from hilltop to hilltop. Stting there,
would I long to be where I am now?

Scenes

WHILE SITTING ATOP A CATLIN HILL MEADOW IN EARLY AUTUMN

valleys and hilltops spread out before
me like a September calendar picture
under a large and semi-circular sky.

Clouds to the west are backlit, their
undersides dark and heavy—the sun
casting off an indirect light upon

fields below turned the color of
brown sugar—having been cut and
baled, leaving large rolls looking

like giant woolly beasts grazing on
the great plains of antiquity. Nearby,
half an ancient maple has split and

fallen to the ground—a sprawled out
old man, having lost his balance over
stones and sticks, gravity dragging

his old bones down to join brother
earth. A bird begins to sing in my ear,
telling me something important—

but stops suddenly, becomes silent,
perhaps remembering his song's a
revelation meant only for ears not

accustomed to the dead of winter.
Here I sit atop a Catlin Hill meadow
in early autumn—knowing that the

days will soon be full of change for
            all that abide.

Scenes

SUGAR HILL TRIPTYCH

STIRRINGS

Late winter and the pond ice
is still thick but pocked
by the warmer rays
of a sun come nigh.

The breeze sings a new
song—though it struggles
against a crow's arrogant
cackle, while water, freed
within the earth, rambles on
about the places it's been—
a story it tells over and
over again until someone
listens with solicitude.

The naked woods snap
and crackle with the
movement of small animals.
Black-capped chickadees
flit among the tiny bones of
sleeping trees like nervous
commuters. It's a day of secret
stirring in a season of unrest.

And does this include the
stirring of hearts who once
lived among these trees,
who sat beside this water,
waiting for the spring to
arrive again?

FOUNDATIONS

Foundations found in the
sleep of winter—slumbering
quietly in dreams of work,
sweat, play and laughter—

Scenes

memories forgotten except
a stranger walking in his
present time finds the objects
of their remembrance:
rusty tools to continue
one's labor in the fields

of heaven and dirt filled
jars to store the meaning
of a once earthly life.

GHOSTS

White birches at dusk—
ghosts walking abroad
among empty cellars—
now holes in the ground
open to an evening sky
filled with pink puffy clouds
trimmed in dusty charcoal.

And here are ghosts walking
among ghosts—all assigned to
hold hands with each other,
forced to finally concede
the sum of things ruled or
possessed never equals
the number of days given
and lived as a gift.

Scenes

WASHINGTON PARK
Thinking of Frank O'Hara's Poetry

1.
Banners in the June sun exhort
me: *Celebrate Washington Park*—
a design of green, ringed in red with
brick row houses under a light blue

sky. So, I exalt the big canopy beeches
with amputated arms and wings like
bats, oaks—solid and heavy with hair
like Medusa, gnarled old maples,

knuckles full of arthritis. I exalt the
locusts with trunks like barber poles,
and the 'tree of heaven' with its ancient
warts and angel wings at the end of its

branches, flying among the star-like
leaves of a nearby sweetgum tree.

2.
I *Celebrate Washington Park* and
applaud Albany's lunch hour ladies
who trade office shoes for sneakers
to stride among mid-day joggers.

Silently, I cheer on the old guys, half
bent over, chatting airily with each
other, while they admire the young
women—quiet and serious in their

runner's ritual, coursing among men
with ties and i.d. badges. I cheer on a
stiff-armed blond with a capacious
behind under a flowered dress.

Should I extol the wannabe beauty
as she appraises the boys with their
big bounding dogs? A cigarette hangs

Scenes

from her painted mouth like an arrow

in a bulls eye. Sure, why not?! I
commend the Albany cops keeping a
relaxed watch over playground kids,
and praise the little black girl gliding

off with dad on training wheels down
a beaten path—heading somewhere
into tomorrow. Here's praying all goes
well on your journey of life. Be safe.

3.
Here at midday in Washington Park,
space and time stop stretching; every
thing holds back for an hour or two.
Even the statue of Robert Burns, with

his floppy hat in hand and fat finger
marking a book, comes alive—a
bemused smile on his blackened-
bronze face as he watches the traffic

flow beyond neatly laid rose beds.
At noon space and time stop stretching
so a quiet man can sit against the trunk
of a towering tree, its leaves shading his

thoughts from the heat of the sun, while
a bare-chested fellow with a pony tail
greedily soaks in its rays through a haze
of cigarette smoke. Everything waits as

two women sit at a picnic table peering
through photos like CIA analysts, while,
nearby, a haggard gray haired joe in a
dirty baseball cap reads a newspaper

Scenes

and picks his nose. Everything waits
until I greet an oncoming giant with a
"how are ya?" and he looks up with a
sudden smile and proclaims,

*Considering this beautiful day—I
would say, definitely, I'm doing good!*

—Albany, NY 2006

Scenes

CINNAMON LAKE SOUNDINGS

Wind journeys through tree tops
like the many voices of a chorus.
Crickets play their fiddles while
songbirds call out the dance.

Dragonflies swing back and forth—
the beat of their wings too fine to hear,
while others drum their tails like
percussionists against the surface

of the water—laying their eggs with
purpose and quite without shame
as other insects buzz and whine like
spirited socializers at a raucous party.

Even if I had to pay for this concert,
surely, it would not have mattered.
For the day is unto itself a song sweetly
sung for the benefit of all nature's soul.

Scenes

ON THE TRAIL TO DUNNING POND

A gentle stream moves slowly
along the trail—its liquid voice
gurgles and plunks its way
across moss covered rocks.

Water spiders glide atop the
calm surface of deeper pools
like Sunday afternoon pleasure
craft on a favorite hidden lake.

Nearby narcissistic ferns bow
down to view their reflections
in the water where a big green
and brown frog pretends not to

notice their hubris. Wood-land
birds, upon a stranger's arrival,
dart from tree top to tree top.
Except for an occasional chirp

or twitter, they are silent and
secretly watchful. At the pond
small fish dart just below the
surface as a noisy kingfisher

heralds the stranger's advance.
A salamander hides on a rock
shelf below the water line, while
turquoise dragonflies hover

above, patrolling their territory.
Just then—not to be outdone, two
fighter jets streak low overhead
as if protecting this pond from
              human intrusion.

Scenes

FIELD NOTES WHILE WALKING BUCK HOLLOW ROAD IN JUNE

I write my wanderings in a notebook
resting on a locus fencepost 'desk,'
which I share with many insects and
a yellow spotted caterpillar—who,
no doubt, puzzles at my presence.

Today, a high wind runs atop these
green hills. A constant rush of sound
issues through trees, shrubs and grass—
all acting as a reed in nature's wood-
wind instrument. A distant roar and a
nearer whoosh form a capacious
symphony in my ear. The wind
suddenly dies to an instant silence . . .
and then, quickly returns.
Even in nature's concert hall, there is
a pause between musical parts.

❋

I then wonder how many insect, bird,
and animal lives are being wrought out
in the thick, grassy pasture waving at
my wandering feet. Which makes me
think of untold lives behind drawn
blinds in faraway cities—all played out
in small, hidden places. Out of site are
most of our stories—no matter their
place and time, never written down,
the majority left behind with the dead—
just like the forgotten family Buck,
who long ago gave its precious name
to this dusty country road.

❋

I notice an oasis of lilac and wild rose—
a way station on the journey of history.
The bones of this homestead lie quiet;

Scenes

it is the way of time and circumstance.
For here a frost-scattered footing of
fieldstone lies buried within the roots
of these bushes—in soil that has lost
its memory of kinship with the family
who once planted in expectancy of
an annual blessing.

❈

Further down the road where a small
stream runs its way alongside, and the
woods are thin and sun-dappled—
a toilet bowl sits like a giant porcelain
mushroom in the wet, mossy ground:
mans' technology meets nature's
running water, and becomes a picture
of contemporary rural America.

❈

I have disturbed a small garter snake
sunning itself in the grass-line by the
stream. He lies quiet as a stick, waiting
for me to compose my jolted thoughts.
What are *his* jolted thoughts as he
warily surveys me—his little pebble-
like head arched slightly above his body,
his thread-like tongue testing the air
between us? Apparently, we have
agreed to be both mutually disturbed
and curious on this summer day—both
man and reptile concurring to move
on to the rest of our respective lives.

Speculations

FOUR SPECULATIONS OF A CONTRARY NATURE

—ON ORIGINS, PERSONHOOD AND SELF

*"David Lewis suggests that we
should have been conceiving of
persons like television shows—
not as three-dimensional objects . . .
but as four-dimensional objects
stretched over a long period of time."*
    —David Kyle Johnson

Did you see my pilot episode
when I slid into personhood
during Auden's *Age of Anxiety*?
Not many did; the ratings were
poor. TV's weren't that common
then—unless you caught it all
while standing with the crowd
in front of an appliance store,
amazed at how realistic it was,
and wishing they could be a
real person like me. It all begs
the question: What came first—
the vacuum tube or the egg?

I couldn't have been much of
a person in my early days;
a radio was all my parents had
for a number of my post-natal
years. And when our first TV set
appeared mysteriously one day
from out of the ether—my
personhood was restricted
to one channel and a weird,
drug-like-kinescope existence.
Considering how I can now be
viewed in high definition color—

Speculations

begs another important question:
Does this confirm or strengthen
Darwin's theory of evolution?

One channel, and black & white
personhood wasn't all that bad.
I trust no one looked down on me
for being an incomplete self.
> (being a self was still
> a viable notion in
> those pre-multi

> media days).
This would have certainly made
an impression on my tender
young ratings and destroyed my
chances at syndication.
As it was, my personhood and
self were renewed for another
year . . . and so on.

One more thing if you don't mind.
Did you see in the latest issue of
TV Guide, my latest existential
crises—including every thought
I've ever had in my mind
> (if there is
> such a thing)
are being made into a new mini
series? Don't miss it; it'll be a
doozy.

Oh, and don't forget to turn me
off after reading this poem. Air
time is getting terribly expensive.

Thanks.
                              Click.

Speculations

—ON DREAMS
(With the aid of Will Shakespeare's "Hamlet")

—*"We are such stuff
As dreams are made; and our little life
Is rounded with a sleep."*

Things get confused during the waking
hours. Though linear, nearly predictable,
we often lack the stuff that clarifies our

observations. We find it hard to carry
ourselves with grace when we enter the
dimension we mistakenly call our *real* life,

the proverbial *here and now*. Critical
thinking seldom precedes our judgment,
thus we never get where "no man has gone

before." A bunch of trees leaves the forest
incognito. In this quasi real life, the so-called
here and now, a man fishes from a small boat.

His feelings are mixed. He's neither happy
or sad. He hardly knows the difference.
Though he's sunburned and catching no fish,

his lassitude is truly heroic, his ignorance—
almost noble: He doesn't realize this make-
believe life will follow its course to a literary
dead end unless he falls asleep soon . . .

In the *dream stuff* in which he is made, the
man fishes from the same boat. His mind
drifts, yet his thoughts are as clear as water:
merrily, merrily, life is but a dream. And
from where he sits, it seems so. Suddenly,

his boat is dragged under the water by a great
pull on his line. Deeper and deeper he goes—

Speculations

until from behind a shadow appears—growing

larger and getting darker, until becoming a
wide-mouth fish, which swallows man and
boat whole in one bite. The man can only

wonder—is this a move toward normalcy or
decadence? For he knows *his little life is
rounded with a sleep* on both sides of his

consciousness, and is not sure of the better.
So, he waits to see which sleep will bring him
favor. At the moment he's alone in the belly

of a fish, and wondering how all this came to be.

—*"And therefore as a stranger give it
welcome. There are more things in heaven
and earth, Horatio, Than are dreamt of
in your philosophy."*

Let's suppose Mr. Shakespeare determined—
when things knock lightly at your door, you
might end up entertaining angels—who,

as strangers, drop off mysterious, fancy gifts
wrapped in tissue paper while on their way
to the hallowed halls of higher conclusions,

where they'll sit in on dusty lectures, tittering
while they hide their faces beneath silvery
wings. After their visit and departure, you'll

pull apart the paper—only to discover the
wrapping is a peony with many ants buried
beneath its petals. These creatures begin to

sing a beautiful melody only your ears can
hear. This is but one of many awards distant
                                    of reason.

Speculations

—*"To die, to sleep, perchance to dream—
ay, there's the rub, for in this sleep of death
what dreams may come."*

Once here in this unknown place, will a little
girl of four in a local fast food eatery—stop
at a table where an elderly man sits, feeding

on his burger, drinking his diet coke, then
offers to shake his hand, and give him a small
hug before walking off with her dad?

Strangers, but strangers no more. Or will he
remain alone forever, never enjoying his
tasteless fries, never exiting his lonely meal?

In such a dream state does a one-eyed waiter
pour water down the side of the glass? Or is
his vision so keen as to see every atom dance?

Can one sing one great song after another,
never droning off key or forgetting the words?
Or, do tongues melt in mouths like snow?

What if in death's dream all the stuff you ever
spilt on your clothes suddenly appeared on
your natty rented tux or little black dress

while at a dinner party held in honor of God?
Perhaps, this will happen in reverse—your
filthy rags folding into splendid array, your

tired dullness becoming acute joy? Consider
all this as you cross the River Styx in a leaky
boat while a giant fish is about to swallow

you whole. It's best to forget about any
desperate oblivion; this is the terminus of
any virtual life. From here on in things get
                                    REAL.

Speculations

—ON PHILOSOPHY

"The greatest philosophers took pains not to be quotable; they expressed their most serious ideas not through direct statement but through implication, allusion . . . irony and context."
— Robert Grudin

When cultivated and credentialed
thinkers earn their living driving
tow trucks while spouting Plato to
fellow luggers of broken autos—
you know the demand for the wisdom
of philosophers, poets and prophets
is at an all-time low.

Some say the age of the intellectual
is dead. Even cats with their knowing
countenance are dismissed as mere
pretenders. No longer are they
considered to secretly hold the
mysteries of this world within
their vertical pupils.

Emeritus professors wander their
houses lost in some Ugaritic myth
while others have turned to carving
birds as a way of making a difference—
just to show how bad it's got in the
area of ultimate questions. Our
time needs a new Kant to redefine

phenomena; a Hegel to loosen the
bonds of confusion; a Kierkegaard to
unravel our postmodern existential
mix. Postmodernism, that bugaboo—
the exhausted end of these modern

Speculations

'isms,' cowering like whipped dogs
with their tails between their legs and

howling at the moon of ultimate truth.
A pensive Dylan wrote, "Many here
among us, feel life is but a joke."
I don't get it; long ago Nietzsche told
us God is dead (apparently without
considering Pascal's wager). Many
still blame a dead deity for the hell

that is their world. Jean-Paul Sartre,
in his Gallic way, left us alone in an
absurd universe with nothing to do
except feel sorry for ourselves.
Wrapped tight in a nihilism of
mental masturbation—we, alone,
certify our existence.
Heidegger, with Teutonic fashion,
said angst is the only way to validate
your reality. Perhaps Karl Jaspers
was right to say we must wait for a
'final experience'. But can we know it
when it arrives? How will I recognize
it from a stay at the Hotel California

or a night in New Jersey? Philosophy
majors drive tow trucks, and most
cats have retreated to sleeping on
the corners of the bed like gargoyles
guarding a medieval cathedral.
Emeritus professors may some day
return from the ancient city of Mari
with stone tablets that contain a
wisdom that tells us if they hadn't
lost their continued existence—
they would have scrapped it all
and started over from the very
beginning. Any questions?

Speculations

—ON SCIENCE

"... you can embrace answers if you're willing to accept the consequences, but the best approach may be to embrace the confusion."
—David Kyle Johnson

Electromagnetism and gravity are wonderful theories and fit nicely in scientific textbooks. However, physics as a whole has missed the boat big-time.

So much for all those atoms, particles and whatnot. They make good conversation on rainy afternoons. Reality, however, is based on grooves like those in a vinyl record.

Many efforts have been made to mislead the huddled masses, but grooves control everything. With a handsome cyclotron made by RCA Victor, scientists can get grooves moving at a snappy seventy-eight rpm. Amazingly, most of the quantum world can be studied at a reliable thirty-three and a third. Yes, it's always been those grooves.

Yet, beware—things get messy when spatial digits lodge alien molecules in the grooves. Reality can spin off the edge and into the void. So much for grooves being safe at any speed.

Speculations

If you're clever enough you can
see why math has little clout; it's
never been about the numbers.
Formulas are just our ignorance
of things hidden well below the
surface. And please get this:

nuclear forces are nothing more
than a smokescreen to hide the
ugly truth the world was once flat.
The gods later rolled it into a
sphere, because they needed a toy
to play with.

Some have tried, but we can't
measure the cosmos's intention—
only the speed and direction it
takes. So, consider: if someone

assumes quarks and not grooves
while shifting into drive, we could
end up like balls of migrating birds—
flying headlong into an alternate
universe, whose history could
quickly tell us, everything we
know is just a joke.

Speculations

DO THE GHOSTS OF OLD FARMERS STILL WATCH THE WEATHER?
A True Tale of Exceptional Time

While walking a country lane,
I came upon an elderly man in
bib overalls, flannel shirt, and
wide brimmed hat, his broad
back turned to me in the late
day sun.

Milking a lone cow in the middle
of a ragged and weedy field, he
sat transfixed on a stool, stolid
like the gray rocks that jutted
from the ground around him.
His brown and white companion
stood equally quiet, her patience
like the erosion of stone.
Watching for a time, I waited for
him to break his ridged pose and
turn, revealing a seasoned face
full of wisdom. Perhaps a glance
toward me would pass on
knowledge long hidden. But no,
his unmoving back was all I saw.

Now I ask: was this scene real
or an apparition, a refraction
of the past stranded in the slanted
afternoon light now filtered via
a mind gone too far afield? Was
it, by some chance, a drifting,
suitable moment meant to
instruct the ignorant present?

And If so, do the ghosts of old
farmers still watch the weather
through misty eyes, feel teats
between their spirited fingers,
elemental weariness in a ghostly
body? I didn't approach nor ask

Speculations

my spectral questions   having
learned to shrug my shoulders
at such audacity. The evening
coming on, I walked away, the
western sky beginning to glow
a luminous red. Not once did I

presume to tell my mysterious
farmer that tomorrow's weather
looked good, at least on this
side of the veil.

Speculations

OUT OF STEP

I believe
it's said by some
we must reach a
point of no desire
if we want
enlightenment.
No yearning...
No wishing...
No longing...
No craving.

However, I find,
even with no
apparent desire
there is still
a need for
its return.

Or perhaps—
to be more
accurate,
objects demand
desire, and an
object will always
be available.

Or perhaps—
when desire
is an empty hole
in the universe,
it sucks up
the surrounding
energy—
leaving little to
show for itself.

Perhaps—
I'll just look
for an object
that will plug up

Speculations

the hole, and then
get back to telling
silly jokes to my
grandchildren.

Speculations

ORIENTATION TO LIFE AMONG THE RUINS

Draw your attention to this enormity:

In this place of disappointment's
exile, moonlight continually falls
upon the ruins of your ambition.
Its cold light may bathe spent

passion in sharp outline—yet, leaves
it with no real substance. The eye
may remain full of invention, but,
what it looks upon are shadows.

Best judge them too difficult to trust.
Please note: in this wreck of a place,
certainty has chosen to close its
weary mind against any faculties.

For living among these ruins finds
one's confidence reeling like a
drunken man in the shifting sand
between aspiration's fallen rubble.

That blood-like roar in your ears is
the fierce wind of denial that blows
between the debris. Too often it
won't allow you to hear the direction

of your heart. To help travel in this
half-light, you can use your fingers
to feel your way through the broken
stones once used to build your

expectations. Be careful though—
their broken edges can cut deep.
Healing balm is hard to find in this
wreckage. Don't depend upon old

maps of your ruined city. What
towers you erected never fell near
their former places, but far away

Speculations

they lie. Whatever streets you

walked before will no longer be
friendly or familiar. Many are
entirely displaced or hidden with a
grimy blanket of frustration. Okay,

listen now . . . despite all this—don't
despair; this exile is not a permanent
address, nor is disappointment a
tenured master. There will be a

Nehemiah to rebuild your shattered
walls and towers. Even tumbled down,
                        they will rise again.

A retired industrial drafter/designer and minister, **T.P. Bird's** interest in poetry began in 1969 when serving in the Army. While stationed at Ft. Ord, near Monterey, CA, he visited a bookstore on Fisherman's Wharf; coming away with a book of poems by Leonard Cohen, Bird got immediately hooked on poetry. As Bird has written elsewhere: . . .*okay—Dylan/was the only poet I knew./Bukowski would come later—/even after I found Cohen's/Selected Poems hanging out on/Monterey's bird-pooped wharf./God bless half crazy Suzanne/ down near the river. And God/bless the anthologies of Hall,/ Hollander and Strand, along/with Penguin's Modern Poets—/plowed like rich soil over chile/in a downtown diner while I/ waited for my hospital shift to begin at Fort Ord.* Now that he is retired, Bird's new vocation is writing (and reading) poetry, now that he has the time to think, life experience, and mental energy to expend. He has a number of poems published in literary journals, and another forthcoming chapbook, *Mystery and Imperfection*, from Kalsey Books. Born and raised in northern PA, he and his wife, Sally, now live in Lexington, KY. They have three grown daughters and five grand-kids.

www.ingramcontent.com/pod-product-compliance
Lightning Source LLC
LaVergne TN
LVHW041557070426
835507LV00011B/1135